Mentally Tough

Boost Mental Resilience, Toughen Up Like Spartan, Master Self-Discipline, and Achieve Your Wildest Dreams.

Nick Anderson

Table of Contents:

Introduction 3
Chapter 1: What is Mental Toughness?................12
Chapter 2: The Difference Between Mental Toughness and Mental Resilience 21
Chapter 3: What's the Big Deal About Being Mentally Tough Anyway?......................................31
Chapter 4: What Exactly Do You Toughen Up?..52
Chapter 5: Mental Toughness is the Foundation for Physical Toughness 68
Chapter 6: Why Do Most People Have a Tough Time Toughening Up?..77
Chapter 7: Develop Spartan-Like Toughness........84
Chapter 8: Toughen Up Mentally With These Drills. 88
Chapter 9: How to Build Mental Resilience.........93
Chapter 10: Effective Ways for Building Mental Toughness..96
Conclusion...98

Introduction

Let's get one thing clear: all of us are frustrated and unhappy with life at some level or another. It's perfectly okay to admit this. No amount of denial is going to make this reality go away.

The truth is, we live in a chaotic world that we didn't create. It's not like we were consulted or asked for permission before we were born into this world. It is what it is. It's filled with disappointment, pain, loss and unhappiness.

The good news is that these form only part of the big picture. Despite all the rough spots, there are lots of places for joy, happiness, contentment and love.

In fact, depending on your mindset, this can be the best world possible. It all depends on how you look at your situation and what you do with what you have to start with.

Not everybody can be born into Bill Gates' family. Not everybody can have the basketball skills of Michael Jordan or Lebron James. Not everybody can be as good looking as Angelina Jolie or George Clooney. For whatever shortcomings your greater reality and your world may bring to the table, there is also a lot to be hopeful about.

However, there is one thing that all of us can agree on: if we want to make our lives now the best it could possibly be, we need to step up. That's right, we need to put in the work.

This is where a lot of people fail. While it's one thing to understand that the life you have is what you make of it, it's another to actually do something about it.

One key reason for this is the fact that too many of us think that we're entitled to the good life. When somebody's entitled, they think that they just need to show up, and the good life is somehow handed to them. They think of it as some sort of door prize like respect, love and acceptance.

Well, if you've been alive for more than a couple of years, you know that that is not true. You have to earn respect and trust. You have to build love.

Outside of your parents, you're not entitled to unconditional love. That's just not going to happen.

Unfortunately, too many of us react in the worst way possible to these basic realities. We say out loud that life is unfair. We feel that we're entitled to somehow, some way, having an easier or smoother life. We imply that life should be fair.

Well, we all know that's not the case. That wasn't the case yesterday, it's not happening today, and chances are, it's never going to happen. That's just the way things are.

We can say that this sucks and there's something wrong with everything and everyone. You're definitely more than welcome to try that.

I suspect that since you're reading this book, you're ready to try another path. This alternative path leads to victory, success, and, believe it or not, greater levels of happiness.

While things will never be perfect, it can come close. Guess what needs to happen? That's right. You need to change.

What needs to change? What about your needs to change?

Short answer? Your mindset. When you change your mindset, you open the door to changing everything about you.

Please understand that most of the things that is happening outside of us are things we cannot control and are things that we did not choose. We can, however, control our thoughts. And these thoughts can lead to better choices in terms of the things that we feel, say and do.

When you start developing more control over the things that you do, you change how you interact with the greater world, and this changes your destiny. In other words, you have changed how you respond to the world around you, and the greater world changes in response.

Please understand that it's a two way street. You can't just sit back and hope and wish and cry that you're not handed the best things life has to offer. You have to earn it. You have to work for it. You have to put in the effort.

Yes, that's right. You have to change. This is how you create and recreate a better world for yourself.

The Worst Part

The worst part (and the scariest part) to all of this is that you need to decide. I'm not talking about getting some sort of "light bulb moment" in your head. Anybody can do that. I'm talking about an actual decision that you're going to stand on no matter what.

A lot of people never get to this point. When you make a firm decision, you're saying to yourself, "I'm going to go through with this all the way. It doesn't matter what side of the bed I woke up on, it doesn't matter how I'm feeling today, it doesn't matter what other people say, and it doesn't matter what kind of setbacks and resistance I encounter along the way. I am in it for the long haul. I am in it to win it."

That's the kind of decision that you need to make. And believe me, this is the scariest thing to a lot of people.

This is why a lot of us are looking around and hoping that somebody out there tries to help us or tries to comfort us, or somehow provide help as we grope our way forward in the darkness.

It doesn't work that way. No matter how well-intentioned people may be around you, it all boils down to what you choose to do with your life and how serious you are in pursuing that decision.

There are too many people out there who are thinking that the world is a very bad place and that their best years are behind them. Well, they're more than welcome to continue to think that way. But sadly, if they don't change their minds, they're going to continue to get the same results that they're currently getting. They reap what they sow.

Please understand that whatever life you're living is the result of the mindset you chose. If you think that life sucks, then guess what will happen? Your life will suck.

If you think that there's a tremendous amount of opportunities around you and you only need to take on the right ones, then you achieve a better life for yourself. It all depends on what you choose to believe and your decision to act according to those beliefs.

This is all a choice. It takes the right mindset to do the best with what we have. The world is never going to be perfect.

Unfortunately, all the pep talk, positivity and mental hypnosis in the world is not going to give you the right mindset. It's simply not going to happen.

If you want to achieve lasting and sustainable personal victory, something else has to take place first. I am, of course, talking about mental toughness.

Have you ever wondered why some people who come from very poor and abusive backgrounds were able to do very well in life? I'm talking about those who lived through horrible childhood sexual, physical and mental abuse.

Regardless of their horrific past, they are well-adjusted and successful. They're happy, and they make those around them happy. How are these people able to do that when there are so many other people with better backgrounds who couldn't do the same things?

There are many other people with better backgrounds, happier childhoods and who didn't need to worry about money, yet they go on to struggle in life. I'm talking about drugs and sex addiction, bankruptcy, toxic relationships and antisocial behavior.

Too many of us may come from privileged and happy backgrounds, but we're walking around like zombies. We're hollow inside. We have no purpose. What's going on?

Well, this has nothing to do with advantages that people either had or didn't have when they were born. Instead, it has something to do with how mentally tough the person is.

Make no mistake, mental toughness is a crucial part of the mental "rehabilitation" people have to go through so they can unlock the relentless winner they have within them.

I hate to break this to you, but you'd be surprised at how much victory you are capable of. In fact, if you truly open your eyes, you'd be surprised as to how many opportunities for victory and success already surround you.

I'm not talking about theory here. I'm not talking about things that could happen. I'm not talking about things that are hidden. I'm not talking about things that may possibly happen with the right support from the right people.

I'm not talking about any of that. You just need to open your eyes and there are already the opportunities for victory in front of you. The only missing ingredient is you.

Whatever riches, potentials and achievements you are dreaming of, it already exists. You don't have to look for it. It's already there. What's the problem? Your mindset.

If you put your right palm right next to your face, what do you see? That's right. Half your field of vision is blocked. But when you move your hand further away from your face, you see everything in perspective.

The same applies to most people. When they're so focused on their problems, their limitations, their past mistakes, their pain, or their loss, they fail to see everything else with the right perspective.

They're so caught up in what they're missing, how inadequate they feel, their loss of self esteem, and all other negative personal judgments that they can't see the tremendous victory, success, happiness, and love all around them.

The more you look at your hand, the bigger it becomes, and the more it blocks your field of vision. The same applies to your problems. The more you dwell on them, the more insecure you feel. You feel that you really can't control much of anything.

Mental toughness enables you to see everything in the right perspective. This book teaches you how to develop mental toughness. This trait will enable you to overcome the kind of blindness that prevents you from living up to your fullest potential.

People may not have said this to you before, but I'm going to say this to you now: You are here for a purpose.

You are not an accident. You are not some afterthought in the great scheme of things. You're not just some bubble that floated to the surface of reality with absolutely no meaning, no purpose and no significance.

You are important. But you have to claim that importance. And the first step is to open your eyes by being mentally tough. That's precisely the skill set you will learn from this book.

Chapter 1: What is Mental Toughness?

Mental toughness is the ability to look at reality for what it is, and not for what you wish it would be.

I know for a fact that most people have been told since childhood to look at the glass half full instead of half empty. That's great and everything, but you cannot stop there. You have to be ready when you find yourself with a glass that is almost all empty. What happens then?

Because that's how chaotic life is. It throws you curved balls all the time. You can't just wish away your problems. You have to recognize reality for what it is without freaking out. That's the difference.

It's one thing to be realistic in such a way that you position yourself for more positive action and better outcomes, and it's a completely different picture when you expect the worst things to happen and your life becomes an uninterrupted chain of self fulfilling prophecies.

Mental toughness involves thinking less emotionally and relying more on logic and reason. If you're having a tough time separating your feelings from your ability to make sense of things, you're going to have a problem.

If you constantly get triggered or you go off on the deep end because you're just so emotionally upset, you're not tapping into your ability to reason through things and detect patterns. In other words, you're bringing a knife to a gunfight.

You're not helping yourself or those around you by being overly emotional and making decisions on a purely impulsive and emotional level. Chances are, you're going to make the wrong call. Chances are, you're not going to get an optimal result.

Being mentally tough means you are tough enough to accurately look at how things are playing out and understand them in a reasonable and logical way.

When you remember things in the past, you're seeking to determine patterns. You're trying to discover lessons. You're not simply reliving a traumatic experience only to feel this surge of negative emotions.

You don't remember things to get that sense of pain, anger, regret and guilt. Instead, you look at the past because you're looking at it as the foundation of better decisions today.

Mental Toughness Involves Making Hard Choices

It's easy to give people the benefit of the doubt regarding certain decisions because we like them. It's easy to choose certain decisions because we're sentimental. But the problem is, if we let emotions get in the way too much, we end up settling for so little.

Being mentally tough enables you to zero in on what you need to do despite the fact that it may tear you up inside.

You may not feel good, you may go against your emotions, but you know it's the right thing. You know that, sometimes, you have to cut in order to heal. Of course, I'm mostly talking about how you process emotions and separate them from logical decisions.

The problem is, a lot of people would rather let their affections drive their decisions. That's why they continue to struggle. That's why they make one bad decision after the other.

A lot of people struggling in battered relationships cannot overcome their personal affection and emotional attachment. You're not doing yourself any favors when your partner is beating the hell out of you while telling you, after they've settled down or when the alcohol or drugs have leveled off, that they love you. Unfortunately, you let your sentimentality and personal affections get in the way.

You have to make hard choices. And the only way to do this is to learn how to become mentally tough.

Mental Toughness Means Overcoming Negative Programming from the Past

A lot of the things that we assume that's true about ourselves is actually an illusion. They are made up. They started off with a kernel of truth, but as time went on, you start reading more and more into them.

We create elaborate grand fables about who we are, what we're capable of, where we can go, where we cannot go, things that we can do and what we cannot do. In other words, we create this identity or internal story based on "past facts."

But when you actually think back to things that actually happened (And I'm not talking about things that you feel, okay? I'm talking about the things that you see, hear, touch, taste and smell. I'm talking about reality.), when you look at this type of fact, verifiable and incontrovertible, what happens?

That's right. It turns out that a lot of those details that you're thinking about, those details that you assume to be true about your past, and which you use for emotional reactions and decisions today, turn out to be false.

At the very best, they're exaggerations. At the very worst, they didn't exist. You just filled in the blanks or you just listened to somebody else's interpretation. It actually didn't happen the way they said it did, and here you are, paying the cost.

Being mentally tough means overcoming this negative programming. How? By being a big enough person to step up and look at the same facts in an unsentimental, uncompromising search for the truth.

If you were to do that, it will turn out that there's a lot of space for a positive interpretation. At the very least, you can interpret these central facts that make up who you are in a more neutral way.

They don't have to make you feel small. They don't have to make you feel powerless. You don't have to feel trapped because you feel that that is just who you are and this is a past that you cannot escape.

Mental Toughness Involves Doing What Makes Sense According to Your Values Instead of Playing to the Crowd

Did you choose to be yourself or did you just "inherit" your identity from the people around you?

This is a hard question to ask because a lot of people assume the answer. A lot of people assume that they are their own person, they are free thinkers, they are autonomous and independent.

Well, try testing that theory every once in a while. You'd be surprised with the results.

The religion that you follow, the political ideology that you use to make sense of news and current events, your ideas regarding personality and the big things in life like love, affection, respect, and value – all of those have to come from somewhere. Newsflash: they didn't come from you.

If you're like most people, you inherited them or you basically just unthinkingly picked up what others have handed over to you. There's almost no resistance. I am, of course, talking about your parents and your relatives.

As you get older, maybe you change a little bit of what they've given you, and then you pick up, again, without question, the things that your friends hand to you. As the old saying goes, birds of a feather flock together.

According to another saying, "I can tell you a man's character based on his friends." There's a lot of truth to that saying because we tend to absorb the values of the people around us.

The problem is, whatever issues you're going through may be due to the fact that you just picked up on these values, assumptions, and world views, without thinking. Do they fit your reality? Do they make sense to you on a personal level? Do they help you get to where you want to go?

Just as it's very hard to put a square peg in a round hole, it's going to be very hard if the values, mindsets, and conceptions of reality of the people around you don't fit your personal reality.

It takes a mentally tough person to realize all of this, and then choose the values, mindsets and perspectives that make sense to him or her. This takes maturity. This takes strength.

Believe me, you're going to raise a lot of eyebrows. In many cases, there may be a lot of emotional drama involved. People might point their fingers.

Don't be surprised if people laugh at you. You might even be called crazy. But you have to be heroic.

The reason why you're facing resistance is because people do not want to be liberated from their mental prisons. The moment they see you step out of that mental cave that everybody's grown accustomed to, how do you think they'll feel?

They start thinking, "At some level or another, maybe I'm living a lie. Maybe the ideas that I'm thinking doesn't fit my personal reality because I'm seeing this guy step out into the light. Well, that can't happen because I don't want to step out into the light. I don't want to feel uneasy about my own beliefs."

This is the root of that resistance. At some level or another, it's not about you. It's about them and the group delusions that they are in.

These delusions take many different forms and come from many different places. We're talking about class, religion, spirituality, ethnic or language groups, gender identity, you name it.

You have to be mentally tough. Because unless you are fully aware of the values that you have and you are sure that they make sense to you based on where you are and where you want to go, you're living a lie.

It's also very inefficient. You are on that life journey, and at the end of the journey you're spent. You're an empty husk. How come? You lived your life pursuing somebody else's dream.

Mental Toughness Means Learning to Cut Your Losses and Admitting Your Mistakes

I don't want to give you the impression from the sections above that being mentally tough means you know the right way from the get go. It doesn't work that way. Usually, reality unfolds in front of you as you go on this journey.

It all starts out dark, regardless of how clear your map is. And as you make your way through that hidden path in front of you, there will be twists and turns. There will be bumps on the road. There will be unforeseen circumstances. Don't be surprised if you make the wrong choices.

Being mentally tough enables you to overcome the feeling that you're emotionally invested in your decisions.

I'm sorry to break this to you, but if you made a wrong call and took the wrong turn, it's not going to help you if you pursue that turn with a lot more energy, focus and strength. You're just going to make it worse.

A wrong turn is a wrong turn. A bad call is a bad call. You have to learn how to cut your losses and admit your mistakes and take a better direction. This takes mental toughness.

History is filled with otherwise intelligent, brilliant, creative and amazing people who are making life so much worse for them and others around them because they did not have the strength to overcome their pride.

Cut your losses. Sure, you feel like a fool, and people can tell. But you're not doing anybody any favors by continuing down that path. Cut your losses, admit your mistakes, and turn.

Chapter 2: The Difference Between Mental Toughness and Mental Resilience

The ability to bounce back after a setback or two is very admirable. In fact, a lot of people look up to others who are able to take a beating and keep on going.

Too many of us are unable to do that. For a lot of people, once they get knocked down, they stay down. They do so, not because they lack strength. They remain down even though they have resources.

A lot of people may have enough time to get back up, dust themselves off, and keep going forward. But they choose to stay down. Most of the time, this is due to a person's attitude.

It's no surprise that we admire people who are able to take a beating from life's circumstances and spring back up. They don't wallow in self pity. They don't stick around more than necessary.

They spring back up from the ground no matter how weak, bruised, battered, and hurt they are. They keep focusing on what they stand to gain instead of constantly looking back to the things they've lost.

It's easy to salute those people. In fact, it's so easy to admire such individuals that we automatically think that they are mentally tough.

This is not always the case. Just because you spring back up and you keep pushing forward, it doesn't necessarily mean that you are going in the right direction or you have the right mindset to eventually succeed.

There are many people who can take quite a bit of punishment as far as their goals are concerned. From divorce, to bad health, to bankruptcy, and everything else you can throw at them, you can count on them to spring back up. Still, despite this amazing trait, they don't achieve their ultimate goal.

How can this be? The answer lies in the difference between mental toughness and mental resilience.

While it's true that most, if not all, mentally tough individuals are resilient by nature, the opposite is not necessarily true. That's right. Not all resilient people are mentally tough. It's one thing to have what it takes to bounce back up, it's another to find the right attitude to do it right.

Think of two boxers. One boxer might be able to take quite a bit of a beating. This person can get knocked down over and over again, but you can rest assured that he will get back on his feet.

But this is a far cry from getting back on your feet and winning the fight. Just because you can spring back up and fight the whole twelve rounds, it doesn't necessarily mean that you will win that match. You have to have the key difference between mental toughness and mental resilience.

The Difference? Positivity

According to Manchester Metropolitan University, Applied Psychology Professor Peter Clough, mental toughness is a "personality trait which determines in large part how individuals deal with stress, pressure and challenge, irrespective of circumstances."

Professor Clough describes a mentally tough individual as "someone who is comfortable in their own skin." This means that they are able to look at challenges and adversities not as dead ends.

They don't view problems as walls that cannot be surmounted or obstacles that will automatically block them. Instead, they view them as opportunities. They're not threatened by adversities and challenges.

This is a very important distinction from mental resilience. You can have the ability to bounce back from all your circumstances, but you do so because you're scared. You're able to bounce back from defeat or even the most crushing setback because you feel that you don't have any other option.

While it's admirable that you're able to get back up, doing so because of fear or desperation is not going to get you to your ultimate destination. Not even close. You have to have a positive outlook. And this boils down to a deep seated sense of confidence.

You're comfortable in your own skin. You feel like you have nothing to prove. You feel like nothing scares you because everything is possible. As intimidating as circumstances may be, you look at them as a puzzle that you can solve.

See the difference in mindset? It is no surprise that mentally tough people are able to get knocked down, but come roaring back because they saw the challenge as a stepping stone instead of a tombstone of their hopes and dreams.

What Makes Up Mental Toughness?

There are many formulations for mental toughness. Different people come up with their own different mnemonics. However, if you break down these factors as experienced by different people from different backgrounds, they boil down to four key areas.

Factor #1: A sense of control

This trait involves your ability to control yourself. Despite what's going on around you, you are able to respond to situations, guided by your values and/or the outcome that you desire. This requires you to look beyond or past two inches or two feet from your nose. You look at the big picture.

Control also indicates your level of confidence in your ability to control how you respond to your circumstances. Self control involves emotions and emotional reactions. External control, on the other hand, involves control over how you perceive what's going on around you.

This is a big deal because how you read external stimuli has a strong impact on your emotional state and the things that you choose to say and do. These decisions can start a chain reaction that can affect your external circumstances.

Factor #2: The ability to decide and stick to it

There are many options in front of you. In fact, in most cases, there are too many options. You have to learn how to decide on a goal that you want and you have to stick to it.

This is not just a simple matter of waking up one day and deciding to become a lawyer, a doctor, or a multimillionaire. Instead, you make a promise to yourself when you decide, and you will then set up milestones that you can verify.

If this sounds familiar, this is goal setting. But the lynchpin here or the most crucial component is your ability to decide and stick to it.

This is not something you take lightly. This is not something that just rolls off your tongue or something you say instinctively. You have to decide only after you have looked at other opportunities and possibilities and decide which fits your values best.

Factor #3: The willingness to go beyond what's comfortable

The first two factors are actually pretty straightforward. In fact, most people can understand and even desire these two factors. What really separates mentally tough people from people who think they're mentally tough and people who are just ill-equipped is the ability to handle challenges.

You have to understand that your ability to decide on an alternate reality and reorganize your life in such a way that you think, say and do things that make that alternative idea turn into a reality, takes a lot of work. It takes quite a bit of commitment. You have to stick to the plan for a long time.

You also have to be flexible. Most people can mentally and emotionally get worked up regarding their sense of control and their ability to decide, but when it comes to the day to day changes and inconveniences and discomforts of getting to their ultimate destination, they fall apart.

If you want to be a mentally tough person, you have to take the initiative in challenging your assumptions and pushing the walls of your comfort zone outward. That's how you mature. This is how you level up.

Factor #4: Confidence built on competence

For the longest time in the United States and other parts of the world, behavioral psychologists and public policy makers were under the impression that children can be taught to be confident through simple affirmation.

The idea is, if you tell a student that he or she is worthy, this self esteem that you're teaching them can lead to confidence. Put in another way, the better people feel about themselves, the more confident they would be, and this would lead to greater life success.

Well, thanks to the research of Professor Roy Beaumeister, the "self esteem paradigm" fell apart like a house of cards. It turned out that a lot of people who have been told that they are worthy, that they're perfect, and that there's nothing wrong with them were ill-equipped to handle life's ups and downs.

They go out there all confident about their ability to shape their reality and they get knocked back. It's not pretty. They then blame other people or circumstances for their failings.

It's not unusual for somebody who's been told their whole life that they are great and there's nothing wrong with them and they're perfect the way they are to experience a setback, and guess what? It's everybody else's fault except theirs. This is not unexpected.

Beaumeister's research showed that truly confident people became confident as they got more competent. In other words, the human mind is looking for objective bases or foundations for self esteem, which then produces confidence. In other words, achievements have to come first, and everything else will flow from that.

When you are able to do certain things right in your life, and you can count on yourself to do the right things to produce the right results, you can't help but feel good about yourself. You feel worthy. You feel competent. You're good for something.

What do you think happens next? Well, you become more confident about certain areas of your life, and you're more likely to engage in those activities.

As you push your boundaries forward and learn more things, you feel even better about yourself.

Until eventually, you reach a calm and mature level of confidence because you've built your self esteem on the firm bedrock of competence.

This competence-based confidence is a crucial component of mental toughness.

Where Does Resilience Fit Into All of This?

Mental toughness consists of all four factors above. However, mentally resilient people only have the ability to make a decision and stick with it, and a sense of control. That's all they have.

They don't have the positivity to look at challenges as opportunities. They don't have the right mindset to constantly challenge themselves so they get better and better. They also don't build the competence-based confidence needed for ultimate success.

It is no surprise that resilience is usually passive. In other words, things happen to you, and then you're able to bounce back.

Mentally tough people, on the other hand, are able to make things happen. And if they make a wrong move or make a bad call, they're able to get back up and keep pushing forward.

Despite the differences between mental toughness and resilience, please understand that you can only build them up through doing. You can't think your way into becoming a mentally resilient person. That's just not going to happen.

The same applies to being mentally tough. You can get all the coaching in the world, but until and unless you apply these principles in your daily waking life, nothing's going to happen.

These four factors cannot be attained through sheer mental and emotional work. They don't happen in a vacuum. They can only arise through lived experience.

Chapter 3: What's the Big Deal About Being Mentally Tough Anyway?

I've already hinted at some of the benefits of mental toughness in the introduction to this book. In fact, if you are reading this book, you probably have a pretty good idea of why you should be mentally tough. After all, you're trying to learn techniques that would toughen you up internally.

It's a good idea to be crystal clear about the full range of benefits of mental toughness so you can stay motivated as you toughen yourself up.

Please understand that this is not going to be an easy journey. All of us struggle in certain areas of our life. And usually, mental toughness is part of the answer.

The problem is, realizing you have issues and certain weaknesses is one thing, going through a long protracted process to actually becoming a new person from the inside out takes a lot of work. It also involves challenges.

This is not the kind of thing that you all of a sudden wake up and realize that you are a brand new person. It doesn't work that way.

To be mentally tough, you have to live it out. You have to be challenged. You have to go through ups and down. You have to overcome hassles, discomfort, and sometimes pain and loss.

Given this process, it's very easy for a lot of people to lose motivation. At first you thought that it's a good idea, but when the going gets rough, what do you think happens? That's right. You quit.

Don't think that this won't happen to you. All of us who go through some sort of prolonged development and a series of learning experiences will be tempted to quit. This is why it's extremely important for you to be clear about the wide range of benefits you get from mental toughness.

By focusing on these as you try to make it each step of the way, you get the motivation that you need to keep pushing forward.

The last thing that you want to do is to go through the process of mental toughening unprepared. Believe me, the challenges may hit you like a ton of bricks. And if you don't know why you're doing it, it would be very easy for you to just give up.

The Benefits of Mental Toughness

Benefit #1: Forgiveness

When you're a mentally tough person, you outgrow the need to repay the injury done to you by other people. This is a big deal. Because if you spend a tremendous amount of your time every day thinking about how people hurt you in the past, you probably won't be able to achieve much with your life.

All that energy could have been devoted to something more productive. But here you are, thinking about how abused you were, thinking about how other people betrayed you, treated you like dirt, and on and on it goes.

I've got some news for you: welcome to the club. All people, regardless of how seemingly privileged their life may have been, experience tough times.

It's very easy to define ourselves based solely on the tough times that we went through. But doing so robs us of the power that we need in the here and now to move ahead.

If you become mentally tough, you would be able to forgive, forgive again, and forgive some more. You quickly realize that you have better things to do.

Sure, you got hurt. Sure, you lost something. Sure, you're wracked with doubts. But think about the big picture. You're not doing yourself any big favors replaying those hurts over and over again and fantasizing about some sort of revenge or vindication.

When you become a mentally tough person, you focus on what's important. What's important is how complete, happy and peaceful you become because of mental toughness.

You refuse to let your past pain and loss, as well as your present difficult circumstances, define you. This is victory. It really is. Too many people can't get to that stage.

Forgiveness, of course, starts with forgiving yourself. You didn't cause yourself to be a abused. You didn't deserve to be abused. If you've been traumatized by your parents splitting up, you can rest assured that you did not cause their separation, divorce or annulment.

Learn to forgive yourself. This is one of the key benefits of being mentally tough.

You have to understand that in this life journey, there is only really one person that you can rely on, and that is yourself. If you refuse to forgive yourself, you are undermining your ability to trust yourself. It's like you're fighting a battle with one hand tied behind your back.

Mentally tough people learn how to forgive themselves first, and they are able to find the power to forgive others.

Benefit #2: You are able to make hard decisions in spite of your feelings

Please understand that if you have a tough time separating your emotions from your thoughts, you are in good company. A lot of people decide based on emotional impulse.

According to a fairly recent study, participants were asked why they made a certain decision. The participants gave all sorts of rational-sounding explanations. They seemed so logical. But the study was structured in such a way that most of the decisions people make were actually based on impulse.

See how this plays out? People will make a decision emotionally, but later on, they come up with all sorts of rational-sounding explanations. Chances are, you're the same way.

Mentally tough people are able to separate their emotions from their rational faculties. You don't necessarily have to like somebody to work with that person. But if it makes sense to work with a very difficult and unpleasant person so you can get ahead in your career, then that's what you need to do.

Sadly, people who can't seem to get out from under their feelings' toxic effect are unable to do this. They focus on what's emotionally easy. They allow themselves to be swayed by strong emotions.

And that's why they remain stuck. They keep making the same bad decision over and over again. They don't fully think things all the way through.

Benefit #3: You are able to think your way through emotionally tough, complicated and convoluted dilemmas

Come on, you can admit it. If you're like most people, you would like the world and all its drama reduced into simple black and white. Welcome to the club. When faced with all sorts of chaos, complexity and nuance, most people would rather have it easy.

Wouldn't life be so much simpler if all the bad guys wore black hats and all the good guys wore white hats? Wouldn't your life be so much more awesome if you can easily tell the people who love you and care for you apart from those who couldn't care less about you?

Unfortunately, we don't live in an ideal world. And just as bad people can be very bad in certain circumstances, they can also be very loving, supportive and caring people in other circumstances.

The sad reality of the human condition is that we are a combination of both devils and angels. No one is a complete saint, in the same way as nobody else is a complete demon. We're all a mix.

And given all this complexity and confusion, there are a lot of dilemmas that people go through. It can be very emotionally tough.

It's very hard to make key decisions, especially when it comes to people you care about the most. All this confusion is definitely at play when you're dealing with any kind of office politics.

When you're a mentally tough person, you will be able to see clearly enough through the emotional fog. You would be able to go against your knee-jerk emotional reactions and make decisions that make sense in light of all the complexity you face.

This is quite a handy skill to have because most people can't make hard decisions, and they fall into habitual patterns that may lead to a lot of emotional certainty, but little else. That's right, they keep making the same mistakes over and over again, and can't figure out, for the life of them, why they get stuck with the same results.

Benefit #4: You are able to separate your emotions from your values and principles – enabling you to live a more principled life

Let's get one thing clear. We all know how we should be living. It doesn't take a rocket scientist to get the idea that we should have high levels of integrity and we should treat others the way we want to be treated. It's generally a good idea to be the change that we want to see in the world.

All of these are commendable. All of these are good. But the problem is, it's one thing to say these things, it's another to actually live by them.

They are principles. And just like with any other kind of principle, they're very difficult to live out. You have to overcome your natural inclinations. You have to overcome the natural tendency to behave in an expedient way.

If somebody's slapping you around, the easiest path to resolution is to simply slap that person or even smack that person. Problem solved. But you know full well that that cycle of violence is probably not going to go away.

You know full well that, in many very difficult situations, somebody has to give and set the right standard, or at least create some sort of opening so both sides can resolve their problems in a deep, meaningful and more permanent way.

Sadly, most of the time, that person would have to be you. And, let's face it, most people don't want to be that person.

When you're mentally tough, you are able to live a principled life. You are able to make the hard decision to suffer the loss now, or to give in painfully now, in the hope that you will be able to work out the situation in such a way that you will enjoy better results next time. This is the principled life.

Everybody can talk about peace, love, kindness, charity, compassion, but it takes a very big person to be the one to sacrifice and take the initial hit to make these things happen. How come? It's just so easy to just react. It's just so easy to just give back whatever life is giving you.

Benefit #5: You are able to live in a more self-disciplined, self-controlled, and self-contained way

As the old saying goes, if you have a tough time disciplining yourself, other people will do it for you. The most common example of this, of course, is working in a dead end job.

If you don't exercise much discipline over yourself, chances are, the kind of work that you do pays very little and burns up too much time. Since you cannot muster enough self discipline to get the skills training you need to get better paying jobs, you keep repeating the lesson over and over again. You feel stuck. You feel like you're not going anywhere.

The most extreme version of this, of course, is ending up in prison. If you can't control yourself enough not to harm other people or commit crimes, then society is going to step in and give you the discipline you don't want to give yourself.

One of the key realities of life is discipline. Because we all know that deep down inside, human beings have an animal aspect. We want something for nothing; we want to take, take and take; we want to get without putting anything in; and on and on it goes. This is basic human nature.

But if you want to be rewarded in life, in any kind of society, you have to control these basic human impulses. This is where self containment, self control, and self discipline comes in.

People who are able to put in the work without demanding instant gratification and instant rewards tend to go farther in life. They're the ones who are able to get advanced degrees like law degrees, MBAs, MDs. They are able to put in the time and the work without asking for instant rewards because they know that their reward will be greater later on. It's a case of basic economics.

Most people are unable to do this because people want an instant reward. That's why a lot of people stop their education right after they get a high school diploma.

Others go a little further and get an AA degree. Others go even further and get a bachelor's degree. Rare indeed are people who get JDs, MBAs, PhDs, and other advanced degrees.

In the United States at least, the rarer your degree, the more money you make or the higher in the organization chart you get. There's a direct correlation between self discipline, delayed gratification, and self control, and societal rewards.

Now, this doesn't apply across the board. There are, of course, exceptions. After all, Steve Jobs and Bill Gates, as well as Mark Zuckerberg, are college dropouts. But by and large, college degree holders make a lot more money than high school diploma holders.

When you practice mental toughness and make it a key part of who you are, you will be able to master yourself to the extent that you can position yourself better to collect more of society's rewards. This doesn't necessarily have to involve money. It can involve respect, social position, status, and overall respectability.

Benefit #6: You are able to pursue your grand vision for life without getting distracted

Please understand that we're all headed to the same place. I don't want to be a downer, and I definitely don't want to depress or discourage you, but you know what I'm talking about. We're going to die. That's all we have in common.

From the richest to the poorest, black, white, yellow, red – it doesn't matter. We're all going to go to the grave. That's what unites humanity. No amount of advance degrees, no amount of money, no amount of social acclaim can make that reality go away.

Now, with that reality firmly established, wouldn't it be great to pack every single moment you have on earth with a sense of purpose?

Believe it or not, if you want to live a happier, more content and more meaningful life, you have to search for meaning. You have to search for purpose in what you do on a day to day basis. It's very hard to do this when you're constantly distracted. It's very hard to do this when you're sucked into all sorts of drama.

When you develop mental toughness, you are able to resist the distraction and focus more on purpose. You focus more on the meaning of why you're doing what you're doing and how it leads to the greater story or explanation of your life. In other words, you start living your life in such a way that is very different from the way other people live their lives.

Other people are by driven by their next paycheck. Others are driven by sex. Others are driven by what other people think. Instead, you're driven by the higher purpose you have set for yourself, and which you are crystal clear on.

Please understand that, oftentimes, the main barrier to success in life is not so much figuring out what to do or how to do it, but determining why and how come. If you're mentally tough, you'll be able to work with a high degree of purpose. And this leads to a greater sense of contentment, meaning, and yes, happiness.

Benefit #7: You are able to overcome the guilt and regret of the past

A lot of people, regardless of how seemingly talented they are, continue to struggle through life because they can't seem to let go. Please understand that unless you have access to some sort of time machine, you can never change the past. You cannot go back there and play around with the facts in such a way that they no longer impact your present.

What happened already happened. The past is past. But the problem is, the more you obsess about the past in terms of your wanting to change it or you crying over it, it just pollutes your present. It just poisons the tremendous amount of opportunities you have now.

Please understand that you cannot put the toothpaste back in the tube. It's already out. You might as well focus on what you can do today. All you have is the present. This takes mental toughness to pull off.

People who are mentally weak may be very talented. They may be very competent in certain areas of their lives, but they only need to think about the past and they're thrown off track.

Maybe they're pointing their fingers trying to blame somebody. Maybe they're beating themselves up. Whatever it is, it's a complete and total waste of time.

The past only exists for one reason and one reason alone: as a source of information you can use to improve yourself.

When you are relitigating past battles, when you are feeling lousy about bad decisions you've made, or you're obsessing about people who harmed you from the past, you're not learning from your past. Instead, you're allowing it to beat yourself up in the here and now. You're not doing yourself any big favors.

Benefit #8: You are able to override worries about a future that is yet to happen

Just as worthless as thinking about past mistakes and failures is the very human tendency to worry about what's around the corner. I can't even begin to tell you how pointless this is.

You have to understand that you have a tremendous opportunity to shape your reality in the here and now. This means all you have is the present. Do a good job. Give it your best.

When you think about stuff that hasn't even happened yet, you are just projecting your fears into the future. And guess what happens? It erodes the quality of your work, your output and your effort today.

It turns out that a lot of the things that you are worried sick about may not even materialize. You're thinking of the worst case scenarios and you end up setting yourself up for failure. Focus instead on what you can control right here, right now.

As awesome and bright, or as scary and gloomy as the future may be, ultimately, we can't control it. We can control how we think, talk and behave today. Focus on what you can control.

Mentally tough people are able to do this because they focus on what they can control and they are focused enough to set things up in such a way that the future works for them instead of against them.

Wouldn't that be awesome? Wouldn't this be a better way forward than getting so sick and tired of worrying that you end up getting hooked on anti-anxiety medications?

Benefit #9: You are able to focus on what's in front of you instead of procrastinating or being lazy

Mentally tough people know that the only thing that they have power over is the present moment.

They know that once a minute passes, that minute is gone for good. That's why they focus on the present moment and do what they need to do to make their desired outcome or goals a reality.

If you're mentally weak, you get terrified of what you need to do. You have your to-do list in front of you, and at some level or another, you're scared of the work that these items require. They require commitment. They take out energy.

Now, if you're like most people, you prefer taking it easy. You prefer the path of least resistance. You're looking for that straight line or shortcut to go from Point A to Point Z.

Unfortunately, there is no shortcut in life, nor are there any express elevators. Instead, you have to take the stairs, and the stairs are long and winding. Many of its twists and turns are very crooked and require a lot of attention and focus. If you slip up, you might hurt yourself.

If you're a mentally weak person, you know what's involved and it scares you. In fact, you get so intimidated that you focus on something else you can do.

Please understand that when you procrastinate, you're not necessarily being lazy. You're just doing something other than what you should be doing. You end up kicking the can down the road and you're not really doing yourself any big favors.

Finally, you can choose to be lazy. Lazy people simply do not have the energy, both on a physical and mental level, to do something. They'd rather just do activities that take up the least amount of effort.

Make no mistake, regardless of what day it is, regardless of what time it is, playing video games instead of rolling up your sleeves and searching the library for 100 sources for a very complicated term paper will always be the easier choice.

Lazy people always take the path of least resistance. When you're a mentally tough person, you find the strength and the focus to concentrate on what needs to be done right here, right now. You're able to do this because you know you only have the present moment.

Benefit #10: You are able to see the value in people and invest your attention on them

Let's get one thing clear. A lot of the people who are dear to us or who we value the most, they didn't start out that way. A lot of the people that mean so much to us take up a lot of work and a lot of time.

Why? They're toxic. Maybe they're obnoxious to begin with. Maybe they have some sort of character flaw. Maybe they have some sort of moral weakness. Whatever the case may be, chances are, it takes time for them to get their act together.

This is how relationships mature. Both partners or participants put up with each other because they're both going on a journey together. And this is a journey of personal growth and development as friends, lovers, partners or family members.

We're all on different tracks while at the same time being on the same path because this path is our relationship.

As you can tell from this description, if you are a mentally weak person, it's very easy to have relationships that are in arrested development. In other words, you are friends with that person up to a certain point.

Past that point, you're not going to tolerate them. You don't even want to think about them because you don't have the time, energy, mental and emotional resources to invest in them. You have enough problems of your own.

Well, the problem is, if that's your attitude, your relationships are not going to mature. They're stunted.

You can have a great time with your friends, and they may be able to refer you to jobs or business opportunities and you can do the same for them, but it will never be as rich, fulfilling and deep as it could be. How come? You didn't properly invest in each other. This takes mental toughness.

Mentally weak people have shallow relationships. I wish you could say that these relationships are just restricted to friendships, but a lot of the times, they're romantic relationships.

How many times have you heard of wives and husbands asking for a divorce because they realized one day that they didn't really know their partner or their partner doesn't really know them?

Please understand that in this world, not all walls can be seen or felt. But they're walls nonetheless. The worst walls, oftentimes, are the ones we find in relationships.

Being a mentally tough person enables you to find the value in the people around you and invest in them as they sort things out and as your relationship matures. This investment takes the form of your most important asset ever: your time.

Please understand that if you don't put time in a relationship, you don't have much of a relationship. It will remain shallow.

The more time you spend with somebody, the more you learn about that person, and the more you learn about yourself in that relationship. And this, of course, requires change.

This opens all sorts of opportunities for both of you to change. This doesn't happen when you just wall people off and say, "Well, I'm going to be friends with you up to a certain degree" or "I'm going to be lovers with you up to a certain degree."

Sadly, too many people settle for these types of relationships. They're not as rich, fulfilling, and meaningful as they could otherwise be.

Benefit #11: You are able to become the adult in your relationship

As I've mentioned above, sometimes it takes time to wait for another person to mature. Sometimes, you're going to have to be the adult.

You have to understand that different people in relationships come from different backgrounds. Some people were abused as children. Others grew up in a very sheltered background, so they didn't really experience the world with all its ups and downs and rude surprises.

Just as one can be emotionally stunted by an early childhood trauma, one's emotional development can also be held back if one wasn't challenged. If you're with somebody who comes from a very privileged background, it's very easy for that person to develop a sense of entitlement in everything.

Now, as you can tell, in this type of relationship, it's very easy for you to be frustrated. It's very easy for you to keep asking,"Why is it that I can get my act together and my partner simply is too immature, too clueless, or simply emotionally numb to grow up?"

Maybe they don't want to grow up.

You have to be mentally tough to be in that relationship because you're going to have to be the adult. You're the one who's going to have to dish out the lessons. You're going to have to be the one to be patient as this person figures it out and gets his or her act together.

I hope I've made my case clear that you need to be mentally tough. The benefits that I have outlined above are not shallow. In fact, they are quite substantial. If you think about it, they are the building blocks of any kind of success in life.

Regardless of how you measure it, maybe you don't measure it in terms of money, prestige and power, but if you want to be successful in life, you need to be mentally tough at some level or another.

It has to be part of the picture, Otherwise, you're just going to be stuck in a situation where you're going to be forced to accept whatever results life drops on your lap. Not exactly an empowering position to find yourself in.

Chapter 4: What Exactly Do You Toughen Up?

Now that we're clear about the need for mental toughness on so many levels, the next step is to figure out what you're going to be mentally tough on. What exactly do you need to toughen up?

This is not a very easy question to answer because the concept of mindset is actually quite slippery. It's a hard concept to grasp precisely because it has many different parts.

These parts are moving. These parts change with time. They also can take different shapes and forms in different contexts you find yourself in.

Regardless, you need to toughen up your mindset. And the best way to do this is to drill down into different parts of your consciousness.

Getting Rid of Limiting Beliefs

One of the most important aspects of developing mental toughness is to get rid of limiting beliefs. Please understand that what you choose to believe about your life, your place in the world, or how the world operates, plays a direct role in your behavior.

Ultimately, your beliefs impact your reality. They dictate what you think is real. They set limits. They impact what you consider to be opportunities or threats.

The problem is, these beliefs or thoughts that you think are true are not created equal. A lot of the beliefs that you hold may actually be holding you back and dragging you down from key realizations that you need to live a better or more effective life.

You need to reconsider or revisit the things that you assume to be true. For example, do you believe that you don't have what it takes to go to graduate school?

You know that your friends are all going to graduate school. You know a lot of them are making a lot more money with an MBA or master's degree, but, for whatever reason, in the back of your head, you have concluded that you're just not cut out for graduate school.

In fact, you may have repeated this message so many times to yourself that you stop questioning it. You just need to be confronted with the fact that some people you met or people you already know are either going to a master's degree program or already have their degree.

Once you detect those pieces of information, your automatic response is, "Well, that's not for me."

Similarly, if you're walking down the street and you see a nice Ferrari roll up, do you automatically say to yourself, "Well, that's a beautiful looking car, but there's no way in hell I would be able to afford that."

I hope you realize what you just did with that type of statement or something similar. You've just condemned yourself from ever owning a Ferrari, or anything expensive for that matter.

Why? You have cut off all possibility of owning that item. You said to yourself, "There's no way I can afford that." You gave yourself a conclusion.

Don't worry, you are hardly alone. People do this all the time. But that's a limiting belief. You flat out said to yourself, "An advanced degree is beyond me, and I'm not capable of learning what I need to learn and doing what I need to do to afford the nice things in life."

Those are the real messages that you keep saying to yourself. And believe me, you can keep repeating this so often that you no longer hear them. In fact, you can repeat certain messages in your head and you're no longer aware of them, but their impact on your life are all too real.

Please understand that if you're completely honest with yourself, there's really not much difference between you and the people you know with advanced degrees. They are probably dumber than you when they started the program.

Or the guy in that Ferrari, he probably did not have a clue when he began his journey of wealth development that led him to afford that car. You probably know more than him, believe it or not. Still, none of this matters to you because you let your limiting beliefs pull you back and drag you down.

Mental toughness helps you get rid of limiting beliefs by questioning them. Mentally tough people don't assume their destiny. They question what they believe about themselves. And they do this regularly.

This is why they seem to operate with no limits, precisely because they don't assume that the things that they believed about themselves are necessarily true. Maybe the things that you believed were true in a certain time in the past, but not now. Now, they're completely useless. Get rid of them.

Choose Your Personal Values

Mentally tough people choose their values. They don't have their values imposed on them. They don't mindlessly import them, kind of like some sort of data dump using software from somewhere else.

Unfortunately, the vast majority of people simply inherit their values from their parents or their family or their friends.

Now, generally speaking, this might seem like a harmless thing. Because after all, everybody does it. The problem is, if you do not look at your personal values closely and take full ownership of them, you fail to unlock their full potential.

If that isn't bad enough, if you are blind to the personal values you have, they may be holding you back. It may turn out that you have no business having those values. Maybe you should have other values based on what you aspire for or based on the outcome that you want for your life.

This is a big deal because if you're not mentally tough, you end up a robot. You respond to life based on values you did not choose.

To toughen yourself up mentally, you have to choose your personal values. What is important to you? How do you think you should treat others? How do you think you should be treated?

This is how you start living a life of purpose. And it all begins with a choice.

Engineer the Character You Want for Yourself

Please understand that there's a big difference between reputation and character. Reputation is what other people assume is true about you. It's as if somebody described you a certain way, and other people kept repeating that description. And for whatever reason, everybody thinks it's real.

Here is the problem: a lie, regardless of how many times it's repeated, doesn't somehow get transformed into the truth. A lie will always be a lie.

Your character, on the other hand, is who you are behind closed doors. You can't help act out your character. This is who you really are.

It doesn't matter whether people describe you that way. It doesn't matter whether people keep repeating your character description. It just is.

Mentally tough people increase their mental toughness by engineering the character they want for themselves. Again, this is all part of choice. Just as you must choose your personal values, you must engineer the character you want for yourself.

Are you sick and tired of being lied to? Are you sick and tired of being fooled? Well, it's a good idea to practice integrity. Make sure that you mean what you say, and say what you mean. Make sure you stand by your promises, and make sure that you always deliver.

Now, here's the rub. When you practice integrity, this doesn't mean that you're just going to sit around and wait for other people to practice integrity on you. No. You do it regardless of how the world responds.

So, in other words, if you consider yourself a loving person, you continue to love, love and love, regardless of whether the world loves you back. If you consider yourself a generous person, you continue to give, give and give, regardless of the fact that everybody else around you seem to want to take, take and take. That is the power of character.

This is how you mentally toughen up yourself because you chose your character. You chose it on your own terms. You chose it based on your values.

Consciously Select Your Destiny and Purpose

Mentally tough people eventually develop a sense of personal destiny. They understand that they are on this planet for some sort of reason. They're not just some people who automatically live one day to the next. Because hey, let's face it, animals do that.

Now, while we're all going to die and we're all going to get sick, and we all share the same ultimate destiny, this doesn't absolve us from the responsibility of shaping and selecting a personal destiny for ourselves.

What kind of meaning do you want your life to have? Are you just the type of person who is going to wake up, go to the bathroom, eat, work, go back to sleep, and repeat the process again and again, thousands of times, until you die? Is that purpose?

Is that destiny? Where is the meaning? Where's the power?

Mentally tough people consciously select a personal destiny and purpose, and focus on it so much that it drives their daily activities.

You're no longer punching a button at a factory. That is just one part of what you do because it's part of a greater scheme of meaning for yourself. You're no longer composing a legal brief for the law firm you work for. That activity is part of a greater purpose for yourself.

Mentally tough people do this because they are able to overcome more challenges. They are able to push themselves further, and this leads to higher and higher levels of competence, which leads to greater levels of self esteem and self confidence.

Analyze Your Personal Narrative About Your Past in a Clear Way That Works for You Instead of Against You

To become mentally tough, you have to reexamine the personal narrative that you believe about your past. If you do this right, you would start seeing the limiting beliefs. You would start seeing the negative values that you have picked up along the way. Sadly, you will also see the kind of negative character or the character flaws that you have.

Look at your personal narrative and analyze it. Break it down. Is there any other way of interpreting it so that instead of it holding you back and dragging you down and working against you, it can somehow push you forward?

Believe it or not, two people can be presented with the same set of facts, but, depending on how they look at those facts, they can either be held back, put upon or harmed, or they can be inspired, motivated and pushed forward. It's your choice.

You still have the same set of operative facts, but you can craft a different narrative. You can craft a different analysis. You can come up with a different story that would work for you instead of against you. This is crucial to mental toughness.

Be Clear About How You Handle the Future So You can Overcome Any Tendency to Worry

I hate to be the bearer of bad news, but when you are worrying, you're not really taking action. You're not really making any positive changes to your life.

The problem with worry is that a lot of people confuse it with action. They think that if they are so emotionally worked up with all these alternative scenarios for the future that they're actually doing something tangible about the task in front of them.

This is all a mind game. Because what you're doing is that you're just diverting a lot of the precious mental resources that you need to tackle problems right now to something else in the future that has yet to happen. It's a waste.

Mentally tough people become clear about what they're mentally doing about the future. This enables them to cut it off and focus on what is important. What's important is the fact that your actions and thoughts lay the foundation for the future. That's how you change the future.

You don't change the future in reverse. You don't think about something that happens in the future, and somehow hope and wish that it will affect you in the here and now. That's not going to work.

That's like trying to control the weather by chewing gum or wearing the right shirt. It doesn't work. There's no connection. You're wasting your time.

Mentally tough people change their appreciation of the connection between their actions today and the future. Not the other way around.

They focus on laying a firm foundation now so that their future shapes up to be something that they would like. That's how mentally tough people shape a better future.

Get Ready For Change

All the process I described above require a tremendous amount of honesty, analysis, destruction, and reform.

I'm telling you, most people are afraid of change. They're afraid of change not because they don't have the money to do it. It's not like they don't have the time. No. The resource that is really taxing for them is overcoming the fear of change.

You have to understand that, as miserable as certain aspects of your life may be, and as limiting as certain elements in your life may seem, it's very easy to fall in love with your shackles. It really is.

You may find yourself in a mental prison for so long that at a certain point in time, you stop seeing the walls and start thinking of the place as home. This is why it's really important for people seeking to be mentally tougher to clearly understand what's involved.

Not only are you going to be analyzing how you think and what you assume to be true, you're also going to have to take action. You're going to have to turn your back on comfortable fictions that you have been repeating to yourself for so long. You're going to have to let go of the false identity that only works to make you miserable in the here and now.

This takes courage. Because a lot of the times, the limiting beliefs that we have are habitual. They are a product of certain circumstances in the past, but we hang on to them like a worn out, useless luggage.

Reforming your mindset has massive implications, but you have to put in the work. Here are just some of what you need to do to mentally toughen up.

Challenge and Change Your Assumptions for the Better

If you're struggling with lackluster results, maybe you're assuming certain things a certain way. What if you change those assumptions? What if you change your expectations?

This takes a lot of work. This also takes a lot of courage because hey, let's face it, better the devil you know than the devil you don't know.

But if you want to get out from under the negative or disappointing results that you keep getting day in, day out, you need to change your assumptions.

These involve assumptions about yourself and your capabilities, assumptions about human nature, about people in your life and people outside of your life, assumptions about new tasks, and assumptions about the nature of work.

You also have to change your mind, or at least reexamine concepts like reward, work, process, paying your dues, and so on and so forth.

Your assumptions, as I have hinted above, impacts your expectations. Because when you assume certain things are true, then you expect a certain range of rewards, costs and benefits. Your willingness to take certain risks are also affected.

So you have to start with the assumptions you have. Are you sure you don't have what it takes to become a doctor? Are you sure that law school is beyond your ability to comprehend new information and process it?

Are you sure that you cannot work towards a master's degree, or you're just making assumptions? Are you sure that you really desire a certain degree or desire a certain job, or are you just running after them because you think people assume you should want them?

Once you do this heavy lifting, you modify your expectations. This is a big deal because your expectations can position you for a life of regret, second-guessing and doubt, or they can position you for greater success, resiliency and insight. It's all your choice.

Expose Unhelpful Biases

As part of changing your assumptions and the expectations that flow from them, you're going to have to explore your life and your mental processes to expose biases.

Maybe you're setting your ways, both in terms of thoughts and actions, that don't position you well. Maybe you have a certain bias about your past.

For example, you come from a certain country. Maybe you have certain biases about your country that impacts your expectations of your opportunities and limitations. Are these grounded in facts, or did you just assume them? Are they positioning you for greater power and purpose, or are they just dragging you down, making you feel small, weak, voiceless, even powerless?

These are biases. Just because you thought about them and they may have seemed to "work" in the past, it doesn't mean that they're true now.

So ask yourself, "What unhelpful biases may I have about my past, my present situation and my future that may be holding me back or robbing me of the kind of success that I am otherwise capable of achieving?"

Blast Your Insecurities

Insecurities are ultimately assumptions or judgment calls we make for certain assessments we have about ourselves.

For example, you look at yourself in the mirror and you can see your physical appearance. Now, most people have two eyes, one nose, one mouth, a pair of ears, but everything else is judgment.

Everybody's different. The spacing between the eyes, the symmetry of one side of the face and the other, the complexion, the shape of the eyes, the shape of the nose, the thickness or thinness of the lips, the elongation of the neck – these are just objective stimuli. They're just numbers.

But people put this all together and they come up with a judgment. They come up with words like beautiful, stunning, attractive, enchanting, ugly, repulsive, repugnant, plain, boring, mediocre. These are judgment calls. Is there any other judgment, or are these the foundations of your insecurities?

Please understand that just because this seems like common sense to you, or that this is just a restatement of plain fact to you, that they impact you in a very profound way. They train you to think in a reactive way.

So you have to get to the root of this. Is the root of them fact, or is there room for an alternative reading? Even if, objectively, you have to conclude a certain way, is there a way to control the impact of that conclusion?

Believe me, I've seen guys who are out of shape and who don't look all that good, objectively speaking, pull in women all day, every day from mobile dating apps to social events.

I wish that I could tell you that these guys have a lot of money in the bank. I wish I could tell you that they roll around in the latest Ferrari model, but they don't. What they have instead is an infectious level of self confidence that women can't help but get drunk on. And it works like a charm.

So think about your insecurities and second guess them. Don't assume that they are true just because you carried them around for so long like a heavy weight. Just because they seemed to be so true in the past, it doesn't mean that they have to be relevant now.

Please understand that your insecurities are training you to think in a reactive way. They're training you to think in a certain way that doesn't really do you any favors.

I Know All Of This is Quite a Heavy Load

In this chapter, I've covered many different steps for mental toughness, and it is a heavy load. But you have to do each step.

The good news is, you don't have to race through all these steps. Just do them one at a time. Pace yourself.

Chapter 5: Mental Toughness is the Foundation for Physical Toughness

By cleaning up your mental house, you position yourself for physical toughness. Please understand that I'm not talking about you getting so physically tough that you can then become the next UFC-MMA champ. I'm not talking about that.

I'm not talking about you getting your mental house in order in such a way that you become the next Manny Pacquiao. That's not the kind of physical toughness I'm talking about. Instead, I'm talking about your body being able to handle a lot more of the punishment that the elements can bring.

Please understand that there is a strong correlation between your mental and emotional state and your medical health. In other words, for you to be tough and hardy outside, you must first be tough inside.

According to a 2015 study out of the University of Tabriz, published in the Research Journal of Sports Sciences, there is a strong correlation between mental toughness and the amount of physical activity study participants could handle.

In the study, 355 students were examined to determine if there's a correlation between levels of physical activity and mental toughness. The students were asked to fill out three questionnaires. One measured their physical activity, the second gave them a diagnostic on mental toughness, and the third took note of their demographics.

According to this study, there was a very strong link between some level of physical activity and one's mental toughness. Indeed, those with significant mental toughness tend to be more physically active compared to students who are just not active physically.

This study seems to imply that physicality can lead to mental toughness, but it can also be the other way around. It can also be that mental toughness enables you to handle more physical punishment and positions you to be more active physically.

Indeed, in a 2017 report out of the Northwest University Institute of Psychology and Wellbeing in South Africa, Professor Richard Bowden reports in the Open Sports Sciences Journal of the correlation between mental toughness and athletes' success.

This cross study research went through 19 peer reviewed articles involving the intersection of mental toughness and athleticism.

Bowden found that, according to this literature, athletes who are mentally tougher tended to participate at higher competitive levels. In other words, they were able to handle more extreme competitions, which manifests itself in more physically challenging situations.

How to Toughen Up Mentally by Changing Your Physical Habits

As I've mentioned above, if you're mentally tough, you can do more physical things. But if you toughen up yourself physically, you can also toughen up mentally. They go both ways. This is not a one way street.

So if you want to toughen up mentally, you can start with physical toughness. To get here, though, you must first focus on your assumptions.

What follows are three mental exercises and four physical exercises. These are lifestyle changes that anybody can make to foster greater levels of mental toughness.

Mental Toughness Drill #1: Stop assuming that your life must be physically comfortable

At this point, you probably have a certain personal preference for climate as well as humidity, light levels, and other physical sensations. Get rid of them.

Don't assume that you have to be in an air conditioned room for you to feel comfortable. Assume that you can be as comfortable in a hot, sweaty and tropical environment as you would in Northern California.

The more you think about this, the more you start assuming that you can physically handle a wider range of environments.

Mental Toughness Drill #2: Stop assuming that you're entitled to a smooth ride just because you decided to do something

Think about the times in your life where you decided to do something and things didn't work out. Are they crystal clear in your mind? Good. What lesson do you walk away with?

Well, the lesson should be that just because things made sense in your mind and you're pumped up about it, it doesn't mean that when you do it, it's a sure shot to success. Chances are, when you try something out the first time, you fail several times before you get it right.

Well, project that and scale that up to the rest of your life. Just because you have decided to do something, it doesn't mean that you're in for a smooth ride. It doesn't work that way.

So apply this to your relationships. Apply this to your work life. Apply this to your school. Apply this to your business.

Assume that there are going to be challenges ahead. Assume that you're going to have to earn your keep. Assume that there are going to be bumps on the road, and get ready for them.

Mental Toughness Drill #3: Expect the worst and prepare for it

Think of the worst case scenario that could happen to you physically. Imagine losing your house. Imagine being caught in a flood. Imagine being in a fire.

Expect the worst. Come up with the worst scenarios and everything else between. Next, prepare for them.

Now, keep in mind that in addition to having a first aid kit, some food and some survival supplies ready, the preparation that I'm talking about is primarily mental. Ask yourself, "If I lose everything today, will I be okay?" The key here is to think about the kind of mindset you need so that regardless of whatever disasters befall you, you would be able to spring back up.

Please understand that I used the word "spring." I'm not talking about gradually clawing your way back up inch by inch. I'm talking about springing back up. That's the difference between people who succeed and people who struggle or flat out fail.

The difference between these two groups of people is not whether they get knocked down because all of us will get knocked down at some point in our lives. The difference that separates us is how quickly we get back up. Winners spring back up.

Did you know that multimillionaires in the United States have, on average, at least one bankruptcy? Think about that for a second. These are people with a lot of money, but they went through a lot of tough times.

Not all millionaires had a smooth ride. Many millionaires have multiple bankruptcies, but they did not let their bankruptcy define them. They did not let their setback define who they are and hold them down. Instead, when they face a challenge and get slapped down hard, they spring back up.

Expect the worst and prepare for it. I'm talking about physical disasters, but mental preparation mostly.

Physical Toughness Exercise #1: Enjoy cold showers in the morning

Make it a habit to take a cold shower first thing in the morning. When you do this, you jolt your system to wake up fully first thing in the morning.

You not only wake up physically, but you wake up mentally. You're ready for whatever hassles, problems and challenges life could throw your way that day.

In an article in the journal Medical Hypothesis published in November 2007, people who adopted the habit of taking cold showers in the morning stimulate a certain part of the brain called the "blue spot."

Researchers have identified this part of the brain as the source of the chemical compound Noradrenaline. This chemical plays a big role in mitigating the effects of depression.

When people with clinical depression were asked to take cold showers in the morning, they presented elevated levels of wellbeing, optimism, and physical energy. It also reduced their fear and physical pain.

If you want to get a quick jolt first thing in the morning so you can feel both physically and mentally tough, start it out with a cold shower.

Physical Toughness Exercise #2: Tap the power of fasting

Believe it or not, when you fast, which means laying off eating for some time, you are able to focus better. This is due to the fact that your body is able to regulate insulin more efficiently.

This period of zero calories also leads to your body processing whatever energy it has stored more efficiently.

In fact, many people who fast report an unexplained surge of physical energy on the seventh day of their fast. This is usually preceded by a very noticeable increase in awareness and mental clarity.

Physical Toughness Exercise #3: Enjoy long spells of total and utter silence

It's very easy to classify this tip as a mental exercise, but it isn't. For you to reach this stage, you have to be physically still.

In your daily activities, you have to set aside a certain amount of time to cease all physical activities. Just drop whatever it is you're doing and just focus on the present moment by simply being quiet.

You're not practicing mindfulness. You're not engaged in any kind of formal meditation. Instead, you just chose to be silent while being physically still. This is enough to just re-center your focus and help you build up or conserve physical energy.

Physical Toughness Exercise #4: Savor the sweetness of simplicity

In your daily physical activities, try to simplify things. Try to take out all the frills and any kind of automation and just try to focus on doing things in the most basic way.

For example, if you normally park really near the elevator at work, try parking a little bit further away from the elevator and then take one flight of stairs. After a couple of weeks, park even further, and then take the stairs up to two floors, and then keep scaling up over time. You'd be surprised as to how you get used to this and how your mind is able to put up with a lot more physical challenges.

This physically and mentally toughens you up. This can also lead to weight loss.

Make no mistake, when you savor the sweetness of simplicity in many areas of your physical life, you stand to benefit in a wide number of ways. You may very well look better, get stronger, and feel so much better about yourself.

Chapter 6: Why Do Most People Have a Tough Time Toughening Up?

Considering the benefits that you get from mental toughness, why is it that a lot of people simply have a tough time with this concept? What's going on?

It really all boils down to our mindset. If your mindset is soft or you expect things to be easy, you're going to have a tough time coping with new situations as well as challenging certain beliefs. It's very easy for you to get thrown off track. It doesn't take much for you to get confused.

Also, if your mindset is soft, your physical limitations are amplified. You're less likely to put up with extreme physical discomfort.

Mental Toughness Requires Inner Calm

The reason most people have a tough time with mental toughness is not because they don't want to toughen up. Most people would agree that we could all use a little thicker skin.

However, the problem is most of us are not internally calm. A lot of this is due to the fact that we assume that life has to be fair.

Well, life is not fair nor is it comfortable. In many cases, life can be quite rough, and I'm not just talking about physical discomfort. Even if you have all your basic needs taken care of and you are in a climate-controlled room with all creature comforts, you can still be very uncomfortable.

You can choose mental and emotional turbulence. That's how important being mentally calm is and, unfortunately, most of us are not calm. Most of us are focusing on the wrong things. We're blowing things out of proportion, and this creates internal mental and intellectual turbulence that ripples into and manifests itself in the form of emotional issues which, you can bet, affect the things that you say and do.

A Little Bit of Calmness Can Go a Long Way

In a 2012 study out of UCLA published in the journal Human Neuroscience, people who have a long history of meditation actually have a higher gyrification. Gyrification or cerebral cortex folding has been associated with faster information processing.

It turns out that when you're mentally calm, you're able to process information faster and this leads to an even deeper level of calm. This makes a lot of sense because if you are not mentally calm and you freak out easily, you blow things out of proportion, and this mental turbulence creates even more turbulence and inner stress.

On the other hand, if people develop mindfulness or achieve state of inner calm, they are able to process the big picture. At the end of the day, they can see that whatever drama they're dealing with in the here and now, it doesn't really matter in the big scheme of things. That's why they can afford to relax. They give themselves the opportunity to let go and move on.

A lot of people who are going through emotional turbulence or simply have the wrong mindset have a tough time letting go. They make mountains of mole hills; they hang onto symbolic victories and otherwise blow things out a proportion and expend tremendous amount of energy on stuff that ultimately doesn't matter.

By Enjoying a Diminished State of Personal Enjoyment and Entitlement, You can Discover What Truly Matters in Life

Another reason people have a tough time mentally toughening up is because they want it all. We want to enjoy everything. We feel that we're entitled to the very best that life has to offer. However, the problem is the more we hang onto this mindset, the less likely we are going to discover what truly matters.

It turns out that you don't need a lot to be happy. I'm not saying that you should give up everything that you own and live in a cave somewhere but, it turns out that according to study after study, material possessions do not permanently make you happy. There's no doubt that when you buy a new trinket or gadget or status symbol, you get a nice burst of self-esteem, contentment, and happiness. However, you get used to it and you end up wanting more and more and more. It's as if your brain has a built-in adaptive mechanism that possessions simply cannot fill.

While it is beyond doubt that when you buy stuff because you have money to buy stuff with, you do get happier. There is joy there. Nobody's disputing that. The problem is it disappears very quickly.

Imagine buying a new BMW and feeling really good because you're the only the guy in your block to own the latest model of a nice piece of German automotive genius. What do you think happens when your neighbors try to catch up with the Joneses and buy their own BMW or to try to one up you by a Porsche or a top-of-the-line Mercedes? Your joy disappears. You're just another car in the crowd and you go back to square one.

Now apply this process to all sorts of trinkets, gadgets and social status items and you now have a clear understanding of why material possessions don't really produce long-term happiness, self-confidence, and assurance.

Being mentally tough means letting go of these crutches because that's what they are. You shift your priorities by lowering your minimal threshold per personal enjoyment. Do you really need to live in a 10,000 square meter house? Can you get by in a 1000 square meter house? Can you get by with something smaller?

Is it essential that you drive around in a top-of-the-line Mercedes Benz or can a Toyota sedan fit the bill? And on and on it goes.

If you're completely honest with yourself, it turns out that diminishing your state of personal enjoyment and entitlement actually enables you to focus on the things that truly matter. You are able to savor life better. You're able to take a deep breath and feel gratitude and appreciation for the things that truly matter in your life.

At the end of day, you have to understand we all go to the same place. It doesn't matter whether you have two pennies to rub together and you're the poorest of the poor or you're the richest of the rich. We're all going to die. That's the bottom line.

The important thing to consider is what kind of life we lived while we had a chance to enjoy the moment. You have to remember that the past is the past, and you have no access to a time machine that will change the facts of the past.

On the other extreme, the future is yet to unfold. The only thing that you really have any control over is what you choose to focus on today. I'm talking about a moment-by-moment consciousness. Shift your priorities. Focus your "mental vision" on every moment. If you have the right mindset, you can quickly realize that every single moment you're alive can bring victory and contentment.

This requires mental toughness because this means you're going to have to operate without strings attached. You're not going to be using crutches, props, or assumptions that everybody agrees on.

You don't have to be somebody else. You have nothing to prove. You have nothing to be guilty of. You have nothing to account for. You just have to focus on what makes sense right here right now without harming other people.

This is toughness because you have to understand that the moment people see that you are no longer dancing to their tune, you can bet you will be a post. At first, people would point at you and laugh. They'll ridicule you. They'll pass it off as a joke.

However, as you make progress and as you make it clear to them that you are absolutely serious, that's when they turn the screws. They ratchet up the pressure. Don't be surprised if they talk behind your back. Don't be surprised if you get called "crazy." Don't be too shocked if people look at you as some sort of misfit.

You have to understand that group delusions gain their power from the strength of numbers. The more people share the same delusion, the more the deluded feel good about themselves because deep down inside they know that something is off. They can't quite put their finger on it. They're not exactly happy, but they at least get some measure of confidence and assurance by looking at everybody else who shares the same delusion.

To be a mentally tough person, to own your own personal reality means stepping away from this, and that is the most threatening act as far as too many other people are concerned.

Chapter 7: Develop Spartan-Like Toughness

The Spartans were Greeks who were the mirror opposite of the Athenians. In our modern world, we tend to lionize and idealize the Athenians. These were Greeks who prized knowledge and wisdom above all else. After all, Athens was where a large number of classical philosophers came from. Whether you're talking about Socrates, Plato, Aristotle and a long list of other important thinkers, Athens is definitely more than well-represented.

Sparta, on the other hand, represented a different philosophy and world view. Instead of looking at wisdom and philosophy to gain a sense of security, the Spartans focused on physical toughness. Located in Southern Greece, Spartans developed a martial culture where boys, as early as 7 years old, were taken from their parents and trained to be soldiers.

The whole idea of becoming a Spartan is to be strong both physically and internally. It may be a shock to a lot of people because due to the seeming backwardness of this emphasis, but the Spartan lifestyle could actually teach us modern people a thing or two about being mentally tough. I'm not advocating that you blindly copy the Spartan lifestyle because there are a lot of really objectionable practices in the whole Spartan mindset.

However, there are certain gems and one of these is developing mental toughness. The essence of the Spartan mindset is to focus on what you have and make do with the little that you have, and the way to do this is to constantly challenge yourself every single day. Do something hard.

This applies in the face of modern-day people because we've been trained to believe that convenience is our top value .That is why there is such a thing as a fifteen-minute pizza delivery. People get upset when a web page takes a few seconds longer to load. That's how short our attention span has become.

Spartans, on the other hand, expect themselves to deal with hardship. They assumed that life isn't fair and that curve balls are around the corner. They also have assumed the worst, and that's why they are very prepared and, oftentimes, they end up winning.

The first to doing this is to resolve to do something hard, difficult, inconvenient, and uncomfortable every single day. This doesn't have to involve physical activities necessarily. This can involve sitting down with somebody and having a very tough conversation.

Chances are among your many relationships there are certain issues that you have been sweeping under the rug or you're otherwise pretending not to care about, but you know that these issues are important to you at some level or other. It's very hard to talk to certain people in your life. Try doing that.

Another thing you can do is to explore the uncharted. Again, this doesn't have to involve going to some sort of wild vacation, discovering an otherwise undiscovered corner of the world. This can be mental and emotional.

Maybe there are certain dark corners of your past that you've been trying to deny or forget. Possibly, there are certain parts of your personality that you'd rather not dwell on. Perhaps there are certain memories that you have that you're trying to paper over or sanitize.

Explore these dark corners. View them with an open pair of eyes and you'd be surprised as to what you would discover because when you ask tough questions of yourself, it may well it turn out that a lot of the things that you assume about yourself to be true are just illusions.

Can you imagine that? There are certain memories that you've assumed to be gospel truth when it turns out they're not true. Maybe you blew things out of proportion or you just read too much into them but, whatever the case may be, they have a negative effect on who you are now, how you act, what you talk about and how you feel about yourself.

All it takes to get out from under all of these issues is to simply ask tough questions of yourself, of others, and explore the uncharted. In other words, become a mental Spartan, and it all begins with your assumptions. If you assume that life has to be fair and smooth and things have to be easy, then you're already a miserable person.

You know that this is not true. It wasn't true yesterday. It's not true today. It will never be the case long into the future. Forget about it. It's not going to happen. So, why hang onto it?

Instead, embrace the hardness of life. If you're able to do this, then you waste less emotional and mental energy trying to gain other people's approval. Instead, focus on more authentic, honest and direct communication. Speak your truth.

I'm not saying that your truth trumps everybody else's because hey, let's face it, all of us have a thing to learn or two. However, it does help to eventually step up and have some courage of conviction to speak your truth. That's definitely much better than trading this personal truth for group approval, which often turns into group delusion.

Chapter 8: Toughen Up Mentally With These Drills.

The US Navy Seals are some of toughest soldiers on planet Earth. They have to be.

Oftentimes, they are sent as the advanced guard to pave the way for larger military operations. Oftentimes, they are sent in the cover of night, and they have move quickly and inflict maximum damage or achieve strategic objectives rapidly. They are the specialists the US military turns to if they need something done quickly and under cover of darkness.

As you can well imagine, being a Navy Seal is very, very stressful. This is why the US government has invested a tremendous amount of money helping Navy Seals quickly deflate and better handle stress. A lot of their work, after all, involves underwater covert operations.

They use his breathing apparatus that doesn't produce any bubbles. That's how stealth and ninja-like the Navy Seals are. That also gives you a good idea of how much stress is involved in that type of job.

The US Navy Seals have a quick stress deflation system. They breathe in deeply and hold it for four seconds, and then they breathe out deeply and hold that for four seconds. They repeat this several times until they achieve a state of calm.

You can do the same. This will mentally toughen you up especially if you are engaged in anything stressful. Use this Navy Seals' breathing exercise to manage your stress.

Mental Toughness is All About Staying in the Present

When you focus your mind's eye on the present, and all you're thinking about is what's happening around you, you're not worrying about the past. You're not trying to be somebody you're not. You're not trying to please other people.

You're just focused on the opportunities around you and you are, believe it or not, becoming more and more aware of just how much you can control your presence.

Take the case of work at the office. You can do things like most other people and just think about how you screwed up in the past. Maybe there was a big project that your boss was relying on, and you dropped the ball. Perhaps you didn't do too well in training and it's haunting you right now because your understanding is spotty. Whatever the case may be, you're wasting all of this effort and mental energy thinking about the past.

Well, you don't have access to a time machine. Those facts are already set in stone. That milk is already spilled. There's nothing you can do about it. However, here you are wasting precious time and, worse yet, mental energy.

What do you think happens as far as your current performance is concerned? That's right. It's not going to be as high as it should or could be. You're making things worse. You end up, if you're not careful, in a negative feedback loop. The worst you feel about the past, the lousier your current work becomes and this becomes a self-reinforcing system, and you get worse and worse.

Don't be surprised if you don't get promoted. Don't be surprised if you don't get that raise that you've been counting on. None of that's going to happen because you're wasting energy.

Be like the Navy Seals. Focus on the present moment. Focus on how things are playing out right in front of you and take that opportunity to challenge yourself to go where you haven't been before. Explore uncharted territories. Ask a lot of tough questions. Be as curious as you can.

Zero in on the present because that's the power you have. You have no power about the future. You can plan and plan and plan but, hey, let's face it, life is what happens when you're making other plans.

Even the best-laid plans with all sorts of statistics and probabilities often fall flat because the future is the future. You can't control it 100%. By focusing on the present moment, you tap into a liberating and exhilarating experience that can keep your grounded.

This has many practical implications. You are able to be patient. You are able to push forward despite little positive reinforcement. You are able to keep applying yourself when it seems that everybody else is discouraging you, laughing at you, mocking you, or flat-out physically resisting you.

Best of all, even if life sneaks up behind you and smacks you around, you're able to bounce back from the floor. You're able to try again despite the setbacks. In fact, you develop a thicker skin. You're able to tolerate worse and worse setbacks and this pushes you to try again and again and again.

At first, you may take a while to bounce up after you have been smacked down, but as you focus on the things that truly matter, and you focus on the present moment and your power in that moment, you find yourself bouncing back faster and faster until, eventually, even if life drops a two-ton bomb on you, you have already resolved to bounce back up.

Sure, the front door may be locked but you're sure to try the roof. If the roof is off-limits, you have your mindset on attacking the house from the back. If that's not happening, then you resolve to go through the basement, and on and on it goes.

In other words, you have become mentally tough. You stop taking "no" for an answer. You stop waiting for the big things in your life because you have to understand either you step up now or nobody else will. You can't just spend the rest of your life of waiting for somebody else to make the move or for things to be "just right."

Mentally tough people are not only mentally resilient but they are impatient in the right way. They know that all they have is the present moment, and they make the most out of it. They don't waste it waiting. They are always preparing; they always have a Plan B; and they're always exploring. In other words, every single moment is a moment of possibility, adventure, and curiosity.

Chapter 9: How to Build Mental Resilience

No discussion about mental toughness would be complete without a clear chapter on mental resilience. You have to understand, as I mentioned in the early part of this book, there is a big difference between a mentally resilient person and a mentally tough person.

If you were given a choice, choose to be mentally tough because, by definition, you will also be mentally resilient. There are many mentally resilient people in the world, but a lot of them are not enjoying the very best the world has to offer because they're not mentally tough.

Sure, they know how to bounce back, but for what? Bouncing back is just one part of the equation. You also have to do other things. You also have to be prepared for other things.

You have to build mental resilience as part of being mentally tough. Why? Not every shot you take will hit its mark. In fact, when you're just starting out with anything, don't be surprised if most of your efforts fall flat. You're paying your dues. There is a learning curve involved. You have to go through that.

Another thing that you have to realize is that success is often not around the corner. In fact, it's not guaranteed.

With all these facts, what do you do? You build mental resilience by first understanding that failure does not have to be your enemy. Instead, it can be a stepping stone. Please keep that in mind.

Failure, setbacks, challenges, and crushing experiences don't have to be your enemies. You can use them as stepping stones instead of tombstones for your hopes and dreams. They don't have to define you.

Resilience is crucial to effective living because it enables perspective, and it also prepares you for the defeats that life can and does bring. But just because life is eager to hand you one loss after the other doesn't mean that you have to accept the loss. You accept the fact, but you can read it as a stepping stone or as a rent or advanced payment for the victory that you have coming your way. It all boils down to your attitude.

How does this work? Practical resilience starts by being emotionally prepared for letdowns.

According to a study published in the journal Personality and Individual Differences in 2013 performed by researchers from the University of Basel in Switzerland, mentally tough people are less likely to be depressed and more likely to be satisfied with life over their lifetime. This is due to the fact that they are mentally resilient.

Please understand what this means. Allow yourself to develop a healthy relationship with failure, loss, and pain. They're part of life. Admit them, accept them, and learn from them. Accept the lessons that they bring and then spring back up. Remember your mistakes and setbacks do not have to define you. They're just part of your personal journey.

Imagine these moments, as unpleasant as they may be, as your periodic payments for eventual success. Just like when you're paying down a big debt that culminates in you taking possession of something, you're going through the same process but, in this case, you are paying down for a better life.

Chapter 10: Effective Ways for Building Mental Toughness

The first step in becoming mentally tough and resilient is to not assume an easy path. Just get that idea out of your head.

Second, make a big deal about being mentally prepared. The more you focus on being mentally prepared, the higher the chance that you will be mentally prepared. Compare this with completely not thinking about it or forgetting about it.

In 2008 study from a joint study from the University of Leeds and University of Hull, the study, which was published in the Personality and Individual Differences journal, showed that among male and female athletes, there was a strong correlation between internal relaxation and optimism. In other words, they look at how these athletes coped with stressful situation. They had different strategies available to them.

According to the study, when one is mentally tough, one is able to cope, and this leads to greater levels of optimism. This also creates a positive feedback loop. Athletes were able to achieve better results because they are more likely to try.

Compare this with people who aren't mentally tough. They feel that they got burned. They feel that they went through hell and back so they don't want to put themselves in that situation again. In fact, they're so eager to avoid the situation that they refuse to learn from it.

If you want to be mentally tough, don't avoid tough situations. Instead, be prepared for them. Just because in the past you had a tough time, it doesn't mean that you have to repeat it. You can be a bit more prepared now.

You may want to mix things up to get better results. By the same token, don't avoid confrontation but be prepared to handle it in a productive and positive way.

Get excited about the opportunity to learn something new regardless of your present circumstances.

Conclusion

The bottom line is simple. The bottom is pretty straightforward. Life is a test. That's all it is. Are you clever enough? Are you resourceful enough? Are you resilient enough?

If you're thinking to yourself, "Well, this is one test I don't want to take," then that's the problem. If you try to ditch the test or you try to use some sort of shortcut or you try to deny it, there's only one thing that we could all agree on: You're going to have to take the test again.

The truth is life is a test involving many levels, and if you're stuck on a level, you get tested again and again and again until you learn what you need to learn to make it to the next level. A lot of people don't want to admit this. A lot of people are uncomfortable with this. However, it is the way it is.

You can stand around and try to imagine it to be something that it's not. You can try to deny it. You can even try to distract yourself but, let me tell you, for every single second you waste focusing on the things that don't matter, obsessing about the past, or being anxious about the future, you end up wasting time and energy.

You could have invested all of that into just living in the present moment, seeing and enjoying the tremendous opportunities it brings, and exercising your maximum control over your personal reality on a second-by-second basis.

I wish you the very best success in your efforts to become mentally tougher and more resilient!

Copyright © 2019 by Nick Anderson

All rights reserved. No part of this book may be reproduced in any form without permission in writing from the author.

No part of this publication may be reproduced or transmitted in any form or by any means, mechanical or electronic, including photocopying or recording, or by any information storage and retrieval system, or transmitted by email or by any other means whatsoever without permission in writing from the author.

DISCLAIMER

While all attempts have been made to verify the information provided in this publication, the author does not assume any responsibility for errors, omissions, or contrary interpretations of the subject matter herein.

The views expressed are those of the author alone and should not be taken as expert instruction or commands. The reader is responsible for his or her own actions.

The author makes no representations or warranties with respect to the accuracy or completeness of the contents of this work and specifically disclaims all warranties, including without limitation warranties of fitness for a particular purpose. No warranty may be created or extended by sales or promotional materials. The advice and recipes contained herein may not be suitable for everyone. This work is sold with the understanding that the author is not engaged in rendering medical, legal or other professional advice or services. If professional assistance is required, the services of a competent professional person should be sought. The author shall not be liable for damages arising here from. The fact that an individual, organization of website is referred to in this work as a citation and/or potential source of further information does not mean that the author endorses the information the individual, organization to website may provide or recommendations they/it may make. Further, readers should be aware that Internet websites listed in this work might have changed or disappeared between when this work was written and when it is read.

Adherence to all applicable laws and regulations, including international, federal, state, and local governing professional licensing, business practices, advertising, and all other aspects of doing business in any jurisdiction in the world is the sole responsibility of the purchaser or reader.

Printed in Great Britain
by Amazon